The Path Back to My Heart and Soul Connection

MAURA LAWLER

BALBOA
PRESS
A DIVISION OF HAY HOUSE

Balboa Press books may be ordered through booksellers or by contacting:

Balboa Press
A Division of Hay House
1663 Liberty Drive
Bloomington, IN 47403
www.balboapress.com
1 (877) 407-4847

Because of the dynamic nature of the Internet, any web addresses or links contained in this book may have changed since publication and may no longer be valid. The views expressed in this work are solely those of the author and do not necessarily reflect the views of the publisher, and the publisher hereby disclaims any responsibility for them.

The author of this book does not dispense medical advice or prescribe the use of any technique as a form of treatment for physical, emotional, or medical problems without the advice of a physician, either directly or indirectly. The intent of the author is only to offer information of a general nature to help you in your quest for emotional and spiritual well-being. In the event you use any of the information in this book for yourself, which is your constitutional right, the author and the publisher assume no responsibility for your actions.

Any people depicted in stock imagery provided by Getty Images are models, and such images are being used for illustrative purposes only.
Certain stock imagery © Getty Images.

Print information available on the last page.

ISBN: 978-1-9822-1015-1 (sc)
ISBN: 978-1-9822-1014-4 (e)

Balboa Press rev. date: 11/05/2018

Contents

Acknowledgements

Molly Ropelewski - Thank-you for designing the cover of
The Path Back To My Heart And Soul Connection

Charles Connor - Thank-you for
spiritually guiding me to complete
The Path Back To My Heart And Soul Connection
and for your unwavering patience and humor

**Lisa Pomar-Brasil, Patricia McNeilly, Abby,
Ladonna, Edie, Geri Smith, & Stef** -
Thank-you your unconditional love,
support, and encouragement

Youssef Karradi - Thank-you for the artwork in
the book and for your smiles and laughter

The Fairy Shaenna Dixon - Thank-you for
helping me stay focused on completing
The Path Back To My Heart And Soul Connection

Jack Lawler- Thank-you for proof reading
The Path Back to My Heart and Soul Connection

Acceptance Of Self

Acceptance of self.
Being able to let go and lay your past on the shelf.
To trust oneself.
Loving yourself unconditionally.
Looking in the mirror and loving herself/himself.

Beneath My Inner Layer

Beneath my inner layers
I reach for inner strength.
There are and always will be the naysayers
We must be the players of our own game
And not seek outside
Answers as we have
Our own inner guidance.

Building of walls

Building of walls of love.
You are the one that picks me up after I fall.
We call on our angels to help guide and give us strength.
My wall of Love comes down when I know I am safe.

Surrender

I Surrender. We can only be the pretender for so long.
Maybe I should put my feelings for you in a Blender.
Put it in the mail and return it to sender.
You are my one and only contender.

Try

We will try and rise above any way we can.
We may even shed a tear or cry.
You may even ask why.
With a deep sigh.
I always say hi.
I fly higher and higher each and every day.

Hearts Entwined

Hearts Entwined.
You are one of a kind.
Don't mind me saying but you are a rare gem to find.
Our past life we can rewind.
Just remind me of how strong we are becoming.

Across The Miles

Across the miles.
Your smiles.
The sunshine that you bring to me.
And so I let it be.
I will trust and follow God's lead.
As we no longer need to control the outcome
And to become better versions of ourselves
until divine union with you
My home sweet home.

Vision

I had a vision of you so long ago.
The separation between us feels like the worst incision.
Co-creating with you is my best decision.
We will bring in a new tradition.
You are always inspiring and sending me lots of ambition.

Yellow Is The Color

Yellow is the color of the sun.
Yellow is the color of the solar plexus
chakra to stand in your power.
Yellow is the beautiful sunflower or dandelion.
Yellow is a strong vibrant color in a rainbow.
Yellow is the color of lemons that
give everyone a zest for life.

Mystery

Our Love is like a Mystery.
We have plenty of past life history.
I know you love watching many documentaries.
My love for you feels like the best electricity.
This poem I am writing is not for publicity
But my true authenticity.

Halloween

Halloween is a time for making a beautiful scene.
Knowing the fun costumes are so keen.
Trick or treaters going door to door for candy galore.
While ghosts and goblins scare
children as they appear mean.
But in the end Halloween is for everyone.
And the magical fall colors are so serene.

Bridging

Bridging our differences.
Bridging out our many gift of tongues.
Knowing the significances of our true selves.
As the many interferences had to play out in life.
Creating patience and tolerance.
To be accepting of our inner and outer appearances.

Green Is The Color

Green is the color of the heart chakra.
Green is the color of the grass and trees.
One of many natures beauty.
Green is the color of the balloon flying
ever so confidently through the air.
Green is the color that is purifying all that is.

Growth

Growing
Reinventing
Outstanding
Welcoming
Transformation
Healing

Wisdom

Wisdom
Introspection
Strength
Defining
Outward
Merging

Peace

Patience
Evolving
Acceptance
Consciousness
Excitement

Love So Close yet so Far

Love so close but yet so far.
In a blue car.
Wishing upon a star.
Loving you ever day from afar.
Bringing me so much happiness in a jar.
I can't contain it in a bottle of tar.

In A Cave

In a cave I hide for you.
The truest of feelings I have for you.
The light brightly shines within the cave.
For me to be brave and pave the way for a bright future.
As I save or engrave this anyway.
Knowing my heart forgave you.
As I always give you a permanent wave.

Wavered

I have never wavered in my feelings for you.
I have savored every bit of conversation we have always had.
Maybe this poem should be flavored in your
favorite biscotti or German chocolate cake.

Whisper

You whisper to me.
Your soul sings to me through your whisper.
It helps guide me in all my actions and to
become more powerful every day.

Music For The Soul

Music for the soul.
Crawling out from under the hole.
Standing Strong and becoming whole.
It was not long ago you opened my heart and soul.
We both know this journey can take its toll.
But you are always worth the poll.

Don't Quit

Don't Quit.
Be still and sit.
Here is your flame that is lit.

Many a nights

Many a nights
I sit and wonder.
I ponder my feelings that are my authentic truth
As there is proof of how I feel for you.
Even if I have to save it, engrave it, or bring it to my grave.
Knowing the depth of my love for you is
the best gift God has given to us.

The Stars

The stars that shine so bright.
They are out of sight.
The one I wish upon for you
Oh there are quite a few
Twinkling in the night sky
Stopping by to say hi.

Love Conquers All

Love conquers all.
We fall and fall.
We may hit a wall.
We shall choose to either stay small or stand tall.
Yet in the end Love conquers all.

My Love For You

My love for you so innocent and pure.
No medicine or Band-Aid could cure the
love in my soul I have for you.
If you are feeling blue
Or don't have a clue
Just remember the sunshine and happiness you bring to me
So just let it be as
God above has a plan for love.
Bless you always each and every day and in every way.

Your Aura Colors Shine So Bright

Your Aura Colors shine so bright.
They are a beautiful sight.
The stars that shine so bright at night.
One might think our connection is rare
like a beautiful kite that soars
In the air with lots of flair.

Heart Connection

We have a unique heart connection.
We could break it down in each section.
I have always been dedicated but my
dedication to you is one of a kind.
We are guided with love and direction.
With plenty of protection as we meet
And resolve our differences at the nearest intersection.
Along the way we have done a lot of self-reflection.
I know how much I love you and all your imperfections.

Tears

I have cried tears for you the first day
We looked into each other's eyes.
Tears to heal
Tears from past life memories
Tears of joy
Tears of separation
Tears of knowing I can be whole with myself
Tears of thankfulness
Tears of knowing how special you are to me.

It is raining

A day that can be whatever you want it to be.
You bring the sunshine on my darkest days.
Every tear I have for you
I shed like raindrops
Hoping one day they turn
Into rainbows and gumdrops
Every mountain we will climb
Every hoop we will jump over
You are my souls truth
You are me
I am you.

I Wait For You By The Stream

I wait for you by the stream.
You are my radiant beam.
You tear down every wall as I may fall and fall again for you.
I am becoming the best version of myself.
With all the feelings I have for you.
I could lay them on the shelf.

Calm

I feel so calm when I am around you.
No this is not written as a psalm.
Maybe I should email you.com.
This was written in our palm so long ago.
We agreed to meet in this life as long
as you do not have a qualm.
I may record this over the intercom.

The Beauty of Innocence

The beauty of innocence.
The sense of joy, peace, love, and wonder.
Beauty lies within.
Your beauty is essence, one that
cannot be denied or forsaken.
To marvel in delight to take flight and
soar into unseen magical places.

You Are My Valentine

You are my valentine.
Sweet as white wine.
My love for you is always hanging on a vine.
Hoping this poem finds you well and fine.

The Eyes

The eyes are the window to our soul.
Mirroring to us our greatest desire.
We may stop to inquire.
The more deep we go
We keep on making a leap
Towards our greatest goal.

You Are Me I am You

You are me.
I am you.
We are Twin Flames
Until the end of time.
You are my soul's truth
Together we will fly higher than a kite.
Into the night sky.
The stars that sparkle and shine are like
the smile on my face when I see you
And when you forever changed my world.

Calling Out Your Name

Calling out your name.
It is not for fame
Not even a game
My dream you came into
No not a lame excuse
We should not feel shame
As my love for you is true
And of nothing shall I be ashamed

You and I Are Twin Flames

You and I are Twin Flames.
You are my home.
You can examine it anyway you like.
With a fine tooth comb.
We could put our feelings in a big golden dome.
But either way it comes back to you
In a written poem.

Twin Flame Love Is One Of A Kind

Twin Flame Love is one of a kind.
Everything you thought your mind ever knew.
Knowing Twin Flames are hard to find.
Your twin flame always brings you peace of mind.
Twin Flame Love is always twined.
We help each other to be one of a kind.

My Sweet Twin Flame Love

You are my sweet Twin Flame.
You cannot blame me.
As you opened my eyes.
You are ever so wise.
You brought the light from darkness.
I am ever so grateful.
It was divine intervention ever so fateful.
Many a night I had always dreamed of you.
Before we met at the school
As there is no rule
Of the love I have for you unconditionally.
And you are the one who is exceptionally
the best twin Flame.

My Heart And Soul

You engulfed my heart with a flame.

My life has not been the same.

We are not here for fortune or fame.

We came here

To live a loving, peaceful, and joyful existence.

You can only tame my heart so much.

But who can blame me

For my heart knows the truth.

Growth

Growth is like a flower blooming.
As our body, mind, and heart are consuming
All the power to be who we came here to be.
The flames may be fuming.
But as we ascend higher and higher may we transform
And keep illuminating our light
And love upon the new earth.

Merging

Merging into our own.
We are always shown to be still
To fill our mind and heart.
We are never apart.
From our emerging selves
Comes from merging with the other.
We shall not smother the flame
But let it grow and merge and not let ourselves submerge.
But be able to grow like a power surge.

Union

As I await reunion with my twin flame.
I become in union with myself and god above.
The love so strong and divinely guided.
It is not just one sided.
We work to unravel the layers like an onion.
In the meantime we are in communion
With ourselves and God.

Love Is Like A Bright New Moon

Love is like a bright New Moon.
Love is sweeter than sugar on a spoon.
We fly away out of our bright and beautiful cocoon.
I look forward to seeing you someday soon.

You Like

You like the color blue.
You like to bike.
Wishing I could tell you
Of my love I have for
You over my mic.

Blue Is The Color

Blue is the color of the sky.
Blue is the color of the ocean.
Blue is the color of the throat chakra.
To be able to speak your authentic truth, be love,
Having faith and trust in God.
Standing in the conviction of who we/you are.

You Whispered To My Soul

You whispered to my soul.
Either way you can measure it with a cup or bowl.
You had my heart and soul so long ago.

Bright As The Sun

Bright as the sun.
Your personality is so fun.
You are my number one.
We have only just begun.
I chase, you run.
Maybe I should become a nun.
No, not so, as I am the lucky one who
met my amazing twin flame.
None can compare as I struck gold just like a home run.

Eye Of The Beholder

Eye of the Beholder.
We lean on each other's shoulder.
Even in the winter when it gets colder.
Maybe I should file this poem away in my office folder.
Or place this in my card holder.

Tide

As the tide rolls in.
I no longer hide.
As the waves I ride
I wait for you by my side.

Be Love

Be Love.
Have Faith in God above.
Anyway our connection
Is like a puzzle.
And grows into pieces that
Fit like a glove.

Coming soon

Twin Flames and How They Change Your World

About the Author

Maura's unique story of finding myself and the journey back to her twin flame. Gaining the personal growth to accept myself and my eternal love. This is my spiritual path to uniting myself to the deepest part of my heart where I gain the purest unconditional love in awaiting the union of my twin flame.

Printed in the United States
By Bookmasters